Images of Modern America

JOHN F. KENNEDY IN NEW ENGLAND

D0778320

Hyannis Port, Massachusetts, officially consists of a post office located next to a seasonal convenience store. Census records indicate there are 193 housing units, of which 144 are seasonal, and the population is 543. One of those happened to be the 35th president of the United States. The Kennedys transformed this tiny little hamlet into an international landmark. (Cecil Stoughton.)

FRONT COVER: Those who knew him best would say that there were few things that John F. Kennedy enjoyed more than being at the tiller of a sailing ship. In 1962, he chose the Coast Guard yacht *Manitou* (Spirit of the Water) as the "floating White House." In this image, he is sailing her in Rhode Island Sound in August 1962. (Robert Knudsen.)

UPPER BACK: It was a month after the death of Patrick Kennedy at just two days old, when JFK and his son John walked Bailey's Beach in Newport, Rhode Island. The two explored a rowboat, which prompted a hug from dad. Those closest to the Kennedy family noted how the death of Patrick transformed the president and brought his family closer. (Cecil Stoughton.)

LOWER BACK COVER (from left to right): The president is driving around Hyannis Port, swarmed by nieces and nephews, a favorite pastime of Uncle "Jack," a nickname of JFK. It has been said that the only time JFK carried any cash was when he would take the kids to buy penny candy in Hyannis Port. (Cecil Stoughton.); The first couple leave the hospital at Otis Air Force Base in Mashpee, Massachusetts, in August 1963. Jacqueline Kennedy remained hospitalized for a week following the cesarean birth of her son Patrick. The couple was captured holding hands, a rare public site. (Author's collection.); The president arrives for Sunday mass at Our Lady of Peace church in Booth Bay, Maine, on August 12, 1962. He arrived by boat to a crowd of about 2,500 who gathered in front of the Boothbay Fisherman's Co-op welcoming him. Selectman Bob Grover told *Booth Bay Register* reporter Diane Randlett in 2012, "The town was so excited to see the president, no one was a democrat or republican that day." (Cecil Stoughton.)

Images of Modern America

JOHN F. KENNEDY IN NEW ENGLAND

Raymond P. Sinibaldi

ARCADIA
PUBLISHING

Published by Arcadia Publishing
Charleston, South Carolina

Printed in the United States of America

Library of Congress Control Number: 2016952612

For all general information, please contact Arcadia Publishing:
Telephone 843-853-2070
Fax 843-853-0044
E-mail sales@arcadiapublishing.com
For customer service and orders:
Toll-Free 1-888-313-2665

Visit us on the Internet at www.arcadiapublishing.com

For William F. Kelly, Dada . . . "I hardly knew ye"

CONTENTS

ACKNOWLEDGMENTS

I am indebted to many for bringing this lifelong dream to fruition. Heading the list is Laurie Austin, the audiovisual archivist at the JFK Library. Her passion for history, knowledge of the subject matter, and drive to be the best she can be went a long way in assisting this effort to be the best that it could be. She is the consummate professional, and I am grateful for her contribution. Maryrose Grossman of the JFK Library audiovisual staff and her ability to "read my mind" brought a more comprehensive view to the project. Thank you to the entire staff at the JFK Library for their joyful assistance and hospitality. Jennifer Quan of the JFK Library Foundation, thank you for your graciousness. John Newberry, your generosity is appreciated. Debi Davis of Berlin, New Hampshire; John Kearns of the Dioceses of Fall River, Massachusetts; and Mike Habrel, thank you for your fact finding. Thanks go to Mary McIntosh, whose recollections were invaluable, and to nieces Cara and Kristi, for providing my summer base. Thank you to Willie and Paula for their inexhaustible support and to Nancy whose courage inspires all who are touched by her energy. Rach, Beth, Boom, Mook, and Jules tolerated and supported dad's trip down his rabbit hole. Working with Ryan Easterling, Caitrin Cunningham, and Erin Vosgien of Arcadia Publishing has been simply delightful. And to Lynda, "I'm never going to lose your precious gift, it will always be that way."

Most the photographs contained herein came from the John F. Kennedy Library and, more specifically, from White House photographers Robert Knudsen and Cecil Stoughton. Knudsen and Stoughton photographs are noted with their last names. Uncited quotes within captions came from the JFK Library in either written letters or oral histories of the attributed individual. Words attributed to Jacqueline Kennedy are taken from her recorded interviews with Arthur Schlesinger.

INTRODUCTION

John F. Kennedy's heritage was rooted in the country of Ireland and in the city of Boston, Massachusetts. His eight great-grandparents, bearing the names of Kennedy, Murphy, Hickey, Field, Fitzgerald, Cox, and Hannon, emigrated from Ireland dating back into the 1840s. Each of them came to the city of Boston seeking the economic opportunity offered in America. His paternal grandfather Patrick Kennedy represented parts of the city of Boston in both houses of the Massachusetts State Legislature from 1884 through 1896. His maternal grandfather John "Honey Fitz" Fitzgerald served in the Massachusetts Senate, represented Boston's ninth district in the US House of Representatives, and served as Boston's 38th and 40th mayor.

Born in the Boston suburb of Brookline, the second child of Joseph P. Kennedy and Rose Fitzgerald, JFK planted his roots in the city of his forbears and in the seaside community of Hyannis Port, Massachusetts. Inspired by trips to the USS *Constitution* as a young boy, Kennedy was drawn to the sea. He once wrote, "I have been interested in the sea from my earliest boyhood . . . My earliest recollections of the United States Navy go back to the days when, as a small boy, I used to be taken to the USS *Constitution* in Charlestown, Massachusetts. The sight of the historic frigate, with its tall spars and black guns, stirred my imagination and brought American history alive for me." His older brother Joe was born in Hull, Massachusetts, a seaside community on Boston's south shore. The little boy, whom they called "Jack," spent times in Hull visiting his Grandpa Fitzgerald in his oceanfront home. It was in 1928 when he spent his first summer in Hyannis Port that his love affair with the sea was fostered, bloomed, and flourished. This love affair would mark him and then define him, and it would last a lifetime.

He has become an icon, which the Oxford Dictionary defines as "a person . . . worthy of great respect and reverence." He has been marbleized by the mind-numbing events of that dark weekend in November over a half century ago. For those of us who were the children of his New Frontier, the images remain sharp, vivid, and clear, crystalized through the prism of time.

It is difficult to tell when one transitions from human to legend to hero to icon. In 25 years as a history teacher, I discovered a phenomenon I call the iconic streamline. This is simply the singular event for which said icon has come to be known. When students are asked what they know about a particular historical person, the responses are almost always the same: Abraham Lincoln "freed the slaves," Rosa Parks "wouldn't give up her seat on the bus," and Martin Luther King Jr. had "a dream." Throughout my quarter century as a teacher, when I asked my students what they know about John F. Kennedy, the answer was virtually always the same: "He got shot."

Icons hover over our history. They are essential to passing on to future generations the foundations of who we are and from whence we came, each one providing a link in the chain of what Abraham Lincoln called our "mystic chords of memory." However, in the creation of historical icons, their humanity is lost. The person gets buried, hidden from the picklocks of biographers. We forget that they were fathers and sons, husbands and wives, and mothers and daughters. We forget that they were imperfect people living in an imperfect world with the capacity for formidable accomplishments and wrought with the human foibles that plaque us all.

This book's nascence lay two generations before I was born and is a culmination of a half century of interest, study, and living. It is rooted in the journeys of John F. Kennedy's maternal grandfather John F. "Honey Fitz" Fitzgerald and mine, William F. "Billy" Kelly.

The Fitzgeralds and Kellys were neighbors in Boston's North End, and as a result, the Kellys were ardent supporters of the political endeavors of Honey Fitz. Kelly was 14 years old when Honey Fitz became the 40th mayor of Boston in 1910, and the excitement of that campaign ignited a political fire that would burn in him throughout his life.

Kelly and the future president first met at the Boston Athletic Association Clubhouse on Exeter Street in Boston. The meeting is chronicled in his oral history at the JFK Library. Kelly's recollections are as follows: "I first met Jack Kennedy with his brother Joe . . . on April 19, 1935. That was the year my cousin Johnny Kelley [different spelling] the older, won the marathon race for the first time. Jack and Joe were with their grandfather to see the finish of the race. The next time I met Jack was when he became a candidate for Congress in the Eleventh Congressional District . . . I sat in on a conference with all the men of the district and plans were formulated to start the campaign. Living in East Boston, I was requested to act as Secretary of the East Boston area." Kelly served in that capacity in Kennedy's first campaign for Congress and his first Senate campaign in 1952. An aficionado of politics in the wards of Boston, Kelly saw something out of the ordinary in the young congressman and always felt he was destined for a higher calling. As Kelly tells it, "In fact the first time I introduced him in the senatorial campaign [1952] in East Boston High School, I introduced him that night as the future President of the United States." Kelly became Kennedy's eyes and ears in East Boston and was in constant contact with the congressman/senator throughout his tenure in both houses. He and his wife, Mary, were present in Washington when John F. Kennedy took the oath of office as the nation's 35th president.

I was a seven-year-old third grader at the James Humphrey School in Weymouth, Massachusetts, through John F. Kennedy's 1960 campaign for the presidency. The excitement generated by the Kennedy campaign was magnified in exponential proportions in the households of the Kelly offspring. Filled with a sense of pride, I was fully cognizant of how special it was that my grandfather knew the man who was running for the highest office in the land. On election night, my dad allowed me to stay up to watch the returns. Although I am not sure exactly how late I made it into that night, I remember running into my parents' room in the morning anxious to hear the news. Although Kennedy's opponent, Richard Nixon, did not officially concede until the afternoon of Wednesday, November 9, my dad declared Kennedy the winner much earlier, and I was elated.

It is with equal clarity and vividness that the veil of sorrow of that woeful November weekend lives in the closet of my memory. Now a sixth grader at that same James Humphrey School, my memory's curtain rises as my class rounded the corner from the playground. Returning to Miss Rygren's classroom, following Mr. White's gym class, we observed Mr. Bryant, our principal, lower the flag to half-mast. He exchanged a few words with Mr. White, and when White returned to the group, he was besieged with the question "Who died?" Somber faced, he simply replied, "Miss Rygren will tell you upstairs." We climbed the stairs, entered our room, and took our seats. Esther Rygren was an elderly lady in the parlance of her time, an old maid who devoted herself to the children who, for decades, came into her charge. Taciturn yet warm, she did not mince words and emitted a quiet strength that demanded and received respect. She entered the room and immediately was beset with the same question, "Who died?" In front of her desk she stood silent, and it became clear to all of us that she had been crying. And as she searched for words that simply would not come, she reached into the sleeve of her dark purple, gray-flecked dress and withdrew a Kleenex. "I'll write it on the board," she said and turned away. She picked up a new stick of yellow chalk, and in the chalkboard's upper-right hand corner, she wrote, in her perfect cursive penmanship, the words that would forever change the world: "Our President."

The school emptied quietly, and a pall of sadness and silence permeated the bus ride home. When that 45-minute ride came to an end, I ran the quarter mile down the hill and gathered in front of the television, with the rest of the country, and watched a nation bury its president.

The killing of his accused assassin, the discrepancies of the Warren Report, and the conclusion of the House Assassination Committee "that President John F. Kennedy was probably assassinated as a result of a conspiracy" has created a cloud of doubt that perpetuates in the American consciousness to this day. The tragic result is that his death, not his life, has tended to dominate his landscape in American history.

These pages contain images of President Kennedy at home. He lived in New England, yet there are those who will argue that his true home was the sea. He was called by it, drawn to it, challenged on it, inspired upon it, and took comfort from it. Coupled with his own words and the words of those closest to him: his wife, his brother Ted, longtime friends and aides Dave Powers and Kenny O'Donnell, army buddies and aides Paul Fay and James Reed, naval aide Tazewell Shepard, secret service agent Clint Hill, press secretary Pierre Salinger, and neighbor and friend Ben Bradlee, these images bring a clearer picture of the nation's 35th president.

His relationship with the sea was no more concisely and articulately defined than on the night of September 14, 1962. The occasion was a dinner at the Breakers in Newport, Rhode Island, as Australian ambassador Howard Beale hosted the president and first lady on the night before the 1962 America's Cup race. The Australian yacht *Gretel* was challenging America's *Weatherly* for the hallowed trophy. The president addressed the gathering, and in welcoming all, he touched upon the fact that all present were drawn by "a common devotion and love of the sea." He then spoke philosophically of why humans are drawn to the sea: "I really don't know why it is that all of us are so committed to the sea, except I think it's because in addition to the fact that the sea changes, and the light changes, and ships change, it's because we all came from the sea. And it is an interesting biological fact that all of us have, in our veins, the exact same percentage of salt in our blood that exists in the ocean. And therefore, we have salt in our blood, in our sweat, in our tears. We are tied to the ocean. And when we go back to the sea—whether it is to sail or to watch it—we are going back from whence we came . . . therefore it's quite natural that the United States and Australia separated by an ocean but particularly those of us who regard the ocean as a friend, bound by an ocean, should be meeting today in Newport to begin this great competition . . . to race against each other and race with each other against the wind and the sea."

Within days following the assassination of her husband, Jackie Kennedy said, "So now he's a legend when he would have preferred to be a man." Already a hero, the man became an icon, and in these pages the man is unveiled, forever young, forever home in New England.

One

The Early Years

Just 11 days before he took the oath of office to become the 35th president of the United States, John F. Kennedy addressed the Massachusetts State Legislature and spoke of his home state: "For 43 years whether I was in London, Washington, the South Pacific or elsewhere . . . This has been my home and God willing, wherever I serve it will always remain my home. It was here where my grandparents were born—it is here where I hope my grandchildren will be born . . . And so it is that I carry with me from this state to that high and lonely office . . . more than fond memories and fast friendships."

Both of John Kennedy's great-grandfathers came to Boston, fleeing Ireland's potato famine of 1847. Both settled in Boston, with the Kennedys in East Boston and the Fitzgeralds in Boston's North End, and both became political forces in their respective communities, as "ward bosses." Two generations later on May 29, 1917, John Fitzgerald Kennedy was born in Brookline, Massachusetts.

Deeply rooted in the city of Boston, Kennedy spent his early summers in the south shore, seaside communities of Hull and Cohasset, Massachusetts, developing an affinity for the sea that would become a personal hallmark. He was nine years old when his father rented a summer cottage on Marchant Avenue in the town of Hyannis Port on the ocean side of Cape Cod. Two years later, the future US ambassador to Great Britain purchased the home, giving birth to what came to be known as "the Kennedy Compound."

It would become the focal point of a family and a political dynasty. It was here they would gather to relax, play, work, celebrate, and mourn.

This photograph was sent to JFK on Inauguration Day. It came from John Grainger of Bath, Maine, the son of Dr. William Grainger, who delivered JFK's father. It was taken in East Boston in 1899 and includes, from left to right, Mrs. Grady (widow of John, who was killed in the Spanish/American War and whose portrait hangs on the wall), Patrick Kennedy (JFK's grandfather, sitting legs crossed), unidentified (standing), Kitty Lally, Dr. Grainger, Frank Lally, Mrs. Grainger, Mrs. Dan Coleman, Dan Coleman, and Ethel Coleman. Kennedy, Grainger, and Lally played "Forty-Five," a card game, on Friday nights for 40 years. (JFK Library Presidents Collection.)

JFK's maternal grandfather and namesake John F. Fitzgerald, a two-time mayor of Boston and member of the Massachusetts Senate and the US Congress, throws out the first pitch for a Boston Red Sox game at the Huntington Avenue Grounds in Boston about 1910. The Red Sox played there from 1901 to 1912. JFK's mother, Rose (first row, third from left), keeps an eye on her dad. (Boston Public Library.)

Joseph P. Kennedy Jr. pauses from giving his younger brother Jack a wagon ride. The photograph was taken on the side of the Kennedy home at 83 Beals Street in Brookline, Massachusetts. The future president was born in a second-floor bedroom of this home on May 29, 1917. The home became a National Historic Landmark in 1966 and is open year-round. (John F. Kennedy Library Foundation.)

This portrait of the three children of Joseph P. and Rose Kennedy was taken in the dunes of Nantasket Beach in Hull, Massachusetts, in the summer of 1920. The future president sits between his older brother Joe and his baby sister Kathleen. All three would meet violent ends: Joe in World War II, Kathleen in a plane crash in 1948, and Jack at the hands of an assassin in 1963. (John F. Kennedy Library Foundation.)

Jack looks ready to row his boat into the waters of Sandy Beach in Cohasset, Massachusetts, around 1923 as swimmers wade behind him, and his sister Rosemary appears ready to lend a hand. The Kennedys summered a few years in Cohasset, and Joseph Kennedy explored purchasing a home there; however, he decided against it when the Cohasset Country Club would not admit a person of Irish decent. (John F. Kennedy Library Foundation.)

There were winter excursions throughout New England for young Jack Kennedy. Here, he is poised and ready to take on the hills of Poland Springs, Maine, in the winter of 1923. Although quite sickly as a child, which saw him endure bouts of time confined to bed, he was very athletic and, as all the Kennedy children, he loved to compete at anything. (John F. Kennedy Library Foundation.)

The fast-growing family outgrew their Beals Street home but stayed in Brookline, moving just down the street to a home on the corner of Naples and Abbottsford Roads. It was in the yard there around 1925 where Jack posed for this photograph on the day he received his First Communion. Written on the back are the words, "Jacky First Communion." (John F. Kennedy Library Foundation.)

The last week of 1925 found JFK (first row, fourth from left) and brother Joe (beside JFK) in Winchendon, Massachusetts, for a weeklong Christmas house party. Toy manufacturer Martin Converse transformed Winchendon into the "Toy Capital of America," and his year-round resort, the Toy Town Tavern, hosted the likes of Thomas Edison, Norman Rockwell, Pres. William Howard Taft, and the young family of Joseph P. Kennedy. (JFK Library.)

It was in the late 1920s when JFK spent his first summer in Hyannis Port. In this photograph, five Kennedys swim in the ocean off their Hyannis Port residence. From left to right, Rosemary, JFK, Eunice, Joe Jr., and Kathleen pause from their frolicking to pose for the camera. (John F. Kennedy Library Foundation.)

A sophomore at the Choate School in Wallingford, Connecticut, JFK sat for this portrait in 1932. It was this year that he became godfather to the youngest Kennedy, Edward Moore. "Teddy," as he came to be known, was born on February 22, and according to Teddy's memoir *True Compass*, the future president lobbied hard for him to be named George Washington Kennedy. (JFK Library.)

The state of Connecticut would provide a rock in the foundation of JFK's life when he entered the Choate School in 1931. Jack, seen at right, had a tough act to follow at Choate, as older brother Joe was considered by headmaster Seymour St. John to be "the natural leader who won respect both in classes and on playing fields." This would prove to be Jack's rebellious period, and academics were not his top priority. From Choate, he wrote his mother, who was pregnant with Edward at the time, and asked, "Can I be God-Father to the baby?" He did become Teddy's godfather. It was at Choate where he met Lemoyne Billings, seen below at left; Billings and Kennedy forged a friendship that lasted a lifetime, as he was a regular visitor to the Kennedy homes in Hyannis Port and Palm Beach and to the White House. (Both, JFK Library.)

In an image that is somewhat prophetic, JFK is the center of this family portrait taken outside their Hyannis Port home during the summer of 1935. From left to right are (seated) Patricia, Robert, Rose, JFK, and Joe Sr. with Teddy on his lap; (standing) Joe Jr., Kathleen, Rosemary, Jean with her arm around her father, and Eunice standing behind him. (JFK Library, Bradford Bachrach.)

Taken in the summer of 1935, Jack fishes a dog out of the waters of Nantucket Sound. Dogs were ever present in the Kennedy family, and this one had slipped overboard during an afternoon sail. Joe Jr. and another canine watch the rescue. (JFK Library Family Collection.)

Following his graduation from Choate, Kennedy attended Harvard University in Cambridge, Massachusetts. It was here where he cultivated a deep interest in political philosophy and international affairs. The image above, taken in 1938 by Harvard classmate and friend Cammann Newberry, is among the earliest-known color photographs of JFK and was taken at the Spee Club on Mount Auburn Street. The Spee Club was a social club at Harvard that was formed in 1852. In an ironic twist, Newberry would become an administrative aide to Sen. Henry Cabot Lodge, whom Kennedy defeated for the Senate in 1952, and he was staff director for Lodge during his vice presidential bid in 1960 as well. At right is a proof of Kennedy's Harvard graduation photograph. (Above, JFK Library, Cammann Newberry; right, JFK Library Family Collection.)

With Europe embroiled in war and its dark cloud hanging over the United States, the summer of 1940 was among the last summers of innocence for America. Above, new Harvard graduate John Kennedy relaxes on the railing of his parents Hyannis Port home. The moment below was captured as JFK (standing right) and his grandfather Honey Fitz (waving) sail JFK's boat *Victura* through Nantucket Sound. A gift from his parents for his 15th birthday, Kennedy sailed this boat as a youth, congressman, senator, and president. Longtime aide and friend Dave Powers wrote that it was "among his most prized possessions." (Both, JFK Library Family Collection.)

Two

From War Hero
to the White House

In September 1940, Pres. Franklin Roosevelt signed a bill instituting the country's first peacetime draft, serving notice to the young men of America that military service was likely in their not-too-distant future. A young man of privilege connected to the highest echelons of political power, John F. Kennedy used those connections to enter the US Navy in October 1941 despite having been initially rejected for military service for a myriad of medical problems, including colitis, a spastic colon, an ulcer, and chronic problems with his right sacroiliac joint. This ultimately led to the deck and command of PT-109. In that capacity, he would meet his date with destiny as a decorated war hero, which ultimately launched his political career in a 1946 run for Congress.

The 29-year-old war hero prevailed, and after serving three terms in Congress, he burst upon the national scene with a stunning defeat of a very popular Republican incumbent, Sen. Henry Cabot Lodge, in 1952. Fighting off the national Republican landslide led by the 442 electoral vote win by Dwight Eisenhower, Kennedy eked out a victory with 51.3 percent of the vote.

A loss turned into a win when, after a floor fight at the 1956 Democrat Convention, Sen. Estes Kefauver defeated Kennedy on the third ballot and was named Adlai Stevenson's running mate. The win came when incumbent president Dwight Eisenhower trounced the Democratic ticket, carrying all but seven states with 57 percent of the popular vote, including 59 percent of the vote in Kennedy's home state of Massachusetts. Kennedy emerged from this experience with his sights set on a 1960 run at the presidency. When he was reelected to the US Senate in 1958 with 73 percent of the vote, his viability as a national candidate was confirmed.

Eleven different candidates garnered votes at the Democratic Convention in Los Angeles in July 1960, and Kennedy emerged with a first ballot nomination. The November election brought one of the closest in American history, with the Massachusetts senator capturing 303 electoral votes and a razor-thin popular vote margin of 49.72 to 49.55 percent over Eisenhower's vice president Richard Nixon. The 43-year-old John F. Kennedy was—and a century after his birth, remains—the youngest elected president of the United States.

John F. Kennedy was sworn into the Navy in October 1941. Assigned to the Office of Naval Intelligence, he continually requested sea duty, and when the opportunity came for consideration as a PT boat commander, he asked his father to intervene on his behalf. Ensign Kennedy impressed Lt. Cmdr. John Bulkeley, who accepted him as one of 50 from over 1,000 applicants. Before moving to his assignment to attend midshipman school at Northwestern University in Chicago, Kennedy was granted leave in July 1942. He spent that leave in Hyannis Port. The image at left is a rare shot of a bespectacled John Kennedy awaiting an opponent's move in what appears to be a rummy game. Below, he stands in the Hyannis Port driveway, poised and ready for his next assignment. (Left, John F. Kennedy Library Foundation; below, JFK Library Family Collection.)

Kennedy's transport ship to the Solomon Islands came under fire from a Japanese aircraft, and the ship's captain was killed. Kennedy's first command was PT-101 before taking command of the PT-109; he is seen standing at right, shirtless, with the crew on its deck. On August 2, 1943, PT-109 was struck by the Japanese destroyer *Amagiri*, splitting the craft in two and throwing the crew into the sea. After 15 hours at sea, 11 survivors made it to a nearby island, with Kennedy towing an injured crew member to land. With the help of a message carved by Kennedy into a coconut carried by local islanders to Allied forces, they were finally rescued on August 8, 1943. He holds that coconut in the photograph at right. He kept it on his desk while in Congress, the Senate, and the White House. (Both, JFK Library Presidents Collection.)

A year later, Navy aviator Lt. Joseph P. Kennedy Jr. piloted a top-secret mission out of Honington Royal Air Force Base in Suffolk, England. On the website Blythburg.net, local resident Matt Muttitt, who was 10 at the time, described what he saw: "The early evening of 12th August 1944 was typical of late summer . . . I watched in horror as the lead aircraft exploded in a huge fireball. I vividly remember seeing burning wreckage falling earthwards. . .The fireball changed to an enormous black pall of smoke resembling a huge octopus, the tentacles below indicating the earthward paths of burning fragments . . . Sixteen years passed . . . a newspaper article began the process of piecing together the story . . . On that summer's day, Joe Kennedy Jr, elder brother of a future United States President, had died." In the above photograph, on July 26, 1945, Jean Kennedy (Joe's youngest sister and godchild) christens the USS *Joseph P. Kennedy Jr* (seen below) while her grandfather Honey Fitz looks on. The christening took place at the Fore River Shipyard in Quincy, Massachusetts. (Both, JFK Library Presidents Collection.)

Lt. John Kennedy (in Boston with Adm. Chester Nimitz, at right) was discharged from the Navy in March 1945, and in April, he went to work for a Hearst publication, the *Chicago Herald-American*. He covered the United Nations Conference in San Francisco, Britain's elections, and then the Potsdam Conference in Germany. Before his discharge, he recuperated in Arizona with his dog Moe; he is seen below with Moe, his sister Eunice, and brother Ted. Ted tells the story in his Memoir *True Compass:* "My brother decided that Moe was getting to be a nuisance . . . he shipped him back . . . for me to look after him. A note fixed to the crate read, my name is Moe and I don't bite . . . Moe bounded out . . . gave me a glancing nip. Dad had been monitoring . . . Ship him back . . . He ordered me . . . I wrote a note back . . . This dog that doesn't bite . . . Bit me, Teddy." (Both, JFK Library.)

Kennedy and Dave Powers (seen at right in the image at left) are pictured on Bunker Hill Day in Charlestown, Massachusetts, the day before the Democratic primary of June 18, 1946. It was a foregone conclusion that the winner of the primary would be the congressman come November, and Kennedy carried the day, defeating nine opponents. Powers became one of JFK's closest friends, was a special assistant to the president, and was the first curator of the JFK Library. In the image below, taken the same day, JFK marches behind the post banner down Bunker Hill Street in Charlestown. Kennedy formed the post in December 1945 and was its first post commander, while simultaneously literally knocking on doors throughout Massachusetts's 11th congressional district, testing the waters for a run at the office and soliciting support from local political leaders. (Both, JFK Library Dave Powers Collection.)

This photograph marks a primary victory celebration in a home. From left to right are Frank Morrissey, Kennedy's grandmother Fitzgerald, Lemoyne Billings (standing with glasses), three unidentified men, Eunice Kennedy, JFK, Honey Fitz, and Boston police commissioner Joe Timulty. Standing behind JFK are Kenny O'Donnell and Helen Sullivan. O'Donnell was Bobby Kennedy's roommate at Harvard and would become JFK's White House appointment secretary and a most-trusted advisor. (JFK Library Presidents Collection.)

On August 12, 1946, the Kennedy family gathers outside St. Francis Xavier Church in Hyannis, Massachusetts. From left to right are Eunice Kennedy, Joseph P. Kennedy, Fall River archbishop James Cassidy, Rose Kennedy, JFK, Honey Fitz, and Teddy Kennedy. This picture was taken at the dedication of the church's new altar in memory of Joe Kennedy Jr., lost in World War II. The altar is still in use today. (JFK Library Presidents Collection.)

John Kennedy won election to Massachusetts's 11th congressional district with 85 percent of the vote in November 1946. He won the seat once held by John Quincy Adams. Here, he poses with his grandfather John F. "Honey Fitz" Fitzgerald at the desk he once occupied in Congress. Honey Fitz was a representative of the ninth congressional district from 1895 to 1901 and the 10th congressional district in 1919. (JFK Library Presidents Collection.)

Reelected twice with little or no opposition, Kennedy visited every city, town, and borough in the commonwealth at least once in his Senate run. Here, he presents 262,324 signatures to Secretary of State Edward Cronin, placing his name on the ballot for US Senate in 1952. Dave Powers (far right) and Claire Murphy look on. Each signee received a thank-you note. (JFK Library, Dave Powers Collection.)

JFK (seated) debates his 1952 opponent, Republican senator Henry Cabot Lodge (at mic), in the Massachusetts State House. The race was as much a clash of cultures as individuals or parties. Lodge, whose great-great-grandfather dined with George Washington, was the embodiment of the old Yankee/Brahmin establishment. Irish Catholic John Kennedy, 15 years Lodge's junior, represented the "newcomers" to the echelons of political power. (JFK Library Presidents Collection, Joseph Manion.)

Kennedy's campaigns were marked with excruciating attention to detail, with the candidate spending 18–20 hour days working, eating cheeseburgers, and napping in the backseat of cars traveling the state. Among those details was an ongoing presence throughout the commonwealth, such as this sign in downtown Wakefield, Massachusetts, in 1952. (JFK Library.)

Robert Kennedy became his brother's campaign manager in 1952. Leaving his job at the Justice Department, the younger Kennedy leaped into his new position and worked 18-hour days. Initially reluctant, he had to be persuaded to take on the task. Author Robert Dalleck wrote of Robert, " 'I'll just screw it up' " he told Kenneth O'Donnell. He agreed to take the job when O'Donnell warned that without him the campaign was headed for "absolute catastrophic disaster. The result . . . the most methodical . . . scientific . . . detailed . . . intricate . . . disciplined . . . smoothly working state-wide campaign in Massachusetts history." The breakneck pace of the campaign required time for some rest and relaxation as well. In these two photographs, the candidate and his campaign manager relax in Hyannis Port during the summer of 1952. (Both, JFK Library, Harry Finkenstaedt.)

Jack Kennedy was born in 1917, the second of the nine Kennedy children. He was naturally closer with his older siblings, Joe (born 1915), his kindred spirit Kathleen (1920), and Eunice. Joe's death in 1944 and the loss of Kathleen in a plane crash in 1948 created a tremendous void in the Kennedy family. That void was filled when Jack decided to run for the Senate in 1952; it became a family affair as sisters Pat, Eunice, and Jean and youngest brother, Teddy, traversed the state of Massachusetts on behalf of their older brother. The campaign drew the younger Kennedy siblings closer to Jack (seen above). Bobby's running of the 1952 campaign began a bond that would grow and intensify into the White House years. Eunice and Pat (with JFK in the photograph below) were very active in the 1952 campaign and shared times in Hyannis Port as well. (Both, JFK Library, Harry Finkenstaedt.)

In the 1952 Senate race, the Kennedy campaign returned to the people that had gained it success in 1946. Among them was William "Bill" Kelly of East Boston. An Irish Catholic native of East Boston and a veteran of World War I, he was East Boston's campaign secretary in both campaigns. In his oral history at the JFK Library, Mark Dalton, the 1946 campaign manager, said of Kelly, "One of the older figures in Boston politics who helped John tremendously . . . a man whom . . . hasn't been given credit for the work he did." In the photograph above, Bill is seen (wearing glasses and smiling) between JFK and an unidentified woman at Boston's Parker House in October 1952. On the right, applauding in a JFK skirt, is Jean Kennedy, and on the left, wearing a fur, is Bill's wife, Mary. Bill returned (below, wearing glasses and second from right) to the Parker House with other secretaries to celebrate the election of Senator Kennedy. (Both, JFK Library.)

Kennedy and Jacqueline "Jackie" Bouvier met at a dinner party at the home of Charles Bartlett in Georgetown in May 1951. With Congressman Kennedy entrenched in his campaign for the US Senate, their initial courtship was, in Jackie Kennedy's word, "spasmodic." Following Kennedy's election to the Senate in November 1952, it intensified, and in fact, in the spring of 1953, the senator proposed to the *Washington Times-Herald* reporter 12 years his junior. Jackie went to Europe to cover the coronation of Britain's Queen Elizabeth on June 2 and, upon her return, agreed to marry the man who was called America's most eligible bachelor. This engagement portrait was taken during the couple's engagement weekend at the Kennedy home in Hyannis Port. (JFK Library Family Collection.)

On September 12, 1953, Jacqueline Bouvier married John F. Kennedy, the newly elected senator of Massachusetts, in what was, without question, the social event of the year, with approximately 1,000 guests gathered at Hammersmith Farm on Narragansett Bay, Rhode Island. In the photograph above, Charles Bartlett and JFK assist the bride down the lawn as Ted Kennedy and JFK's college roommate Torby McDonald (far right) observe. At left, Jackie prepares to toss her bouquet from the steps. In tapes of Arthur Schlesinger's interviews with Jackie, released in 2011, she was asked when JFK began thinking of the presidency: "Certainly before I knew him . . . the first year we were married I heard him talking with his father in a room at the Cape . . . he never stopped at any plateau . . . he was always moving on to something higher." (JFK Library.)

John Kennedy's bid for the presidency began at the 1956 convention; as Jackie said in the Schlesinger tapes: "After the vice presidential thing, he was definitely aiming for the presidency." Jackie and Jack ride through downtown Framingham, Massachusetts, during the Columbus Day parade in 1958. (JFK Library.)

Sen. John F. Kennedy's campaign in 1958 did not just appeal to those of voting age. He visited schools and implored the students to go home and make sure they told their parents to vote in the upcoming election. In this photograph the Senator and Jackie Kennedy watch a youngster at an elementary school in Webster, Massachusetts, demonstrate how to use the newly invented hula hoop. (JFK Library.)

Ted Kennedy managed his brother's Senate campaign in 1958. The outcome of the election was never really in doubt, but it was essential to Kennedy to win by the largest margin possible to maintain his viability as presidential timber in 1960. Ted Kennedy wrote, "Our biggest challenge was overcoming the apathy of people who thought Jack was a shoo-in . . . but . . . the margin is what counted . . . So we focused on generating turnout." Jackie said to Arthur Schlesinger, "It was the hardest campaign ever." These two photographs were taken in downtown Plymouth, Massachusetts, in October 1958, as the candidate encourages voters to go to the polls in November. The incumbent prevailed against Vincent Celeste, whom he had defeated for Congress in 1950. He received 73 percent of the vote, and his quest for the presidency was on the horizon. (Both, JFK Library, Robert Goshgarian.)

The first presidential primary of the year was held in New Hampshire on March 8, 1960. There were five viable candidates in consideration for the Democratic top spot: Kennedy, Texas senator Lyndon Johnson, Missouri senator Stuart Symington, Minnesota senator Hubert Humphrey, and former Illinois governor Adlai Stevenson. Stevenson had been defeated by Dwight Eisenhower in both 1952 and 1956. None were on the New Hampshire ballot, and in fact, Symington, Johnson, and Stevenson did not enter one primary. This did not stop JFK from campaigning; arriving two days before the primary vote, he gathers with voters in Nashua in the above photograph, where he is signing an autograph. At right, he takes a seat in a dog sled in Berlin, New Hampshire. The sled belonged to Mrs. Milton Seely, who traveled to Berlin by dogsled to work for Kennedy. (Both, JFK Library.)

With the nomination secured, it was off to Hyannis Port to relax and recharge. However, this visit was different than any other previous time spent on Kennedy's beloved Cape, for the entire world was now watching. Not only did throngs of photographers and journalists gather to follow and chronicle his every move, but tourists gathered as well, hoping to catch a glimpse of the future president at home. Jack and Bobby began the task of uniting the post-convention party and laying the groundwork for the race to November, but even the omnipresent demands of the campaign could not keep Kennedy from stealing treasured moments on the sea. In the above photograph, he and Jackie make their way to board the *Marlin*, seen below, for an interlude with Nantucket Sound. (Both, JFK Library, Nelson Tiffany.)

The last day of the campaign was spent at home in New England, with appearances in all six states. The last Gallup Poll showed a virtual dead heat with Kennedy at 50.5 percent to Nixon's 49.5. Here, he greets a crowd of 10,000 at Lewiston City Park in Lewiston, Maine. Maine, which had voted for a Republican president in every election since 1856, did again, as Richard Nixon received 57 percent of the vote. (JFK Library.)

A visit to Vermont's capital city of Burlington could not buck that state's historical trend either. Having not voted for a Democrat for president since 1856, it also went into the column for Nixon, giving him 58.6 percent of their votes; one of Nixon's largest state pluralities. (JFK Library.)

In Connecticut, there was a different story. Kennedy addressed a crowd estimated at 50,000 from the portico of the *Hartford Times* in the Constitution State's capital city. Like all of the New England states, Connecticut had voted for Eisenhower and Nixon in 1952 and 1956. However, in 1960, they gave Kennedy 53.7 percent of their votes and all seven of their electoral votes. (JFK Library.)

JFK speaks from the steps of city hall in Providence, Rhode Island: "I ask you to lead the way tomorrow . . . 100 years ago Abraham Lincoln wrote . . . 'I know there is a God . . . I see the storm coming, and I know His hand is in it . . . if He has a part for me . . . I am ready'. . . 100 years later . . . we see the storm coming . . . if He has a part for us . . . we are ready." Rhode Island led the way, giving JFK his largest plurality—63.6 percent of their vote. (JFK Library.)

A crowd of 8,000 people gathered at Victory Park in Manchester, New Hampshire, as Kennedy appeared with his sisters Pat and Eunice. He answered questions about Castro, the communists, his religion, the budget, the future of colleges, foreign policy, and world peace. As enthusiastic as the crowd was, New Hampshire fell into the Nixon column the next day with 53.4 percent of the vote. (JFK Library.)

The 1960 campaign ended at the Boston Garden in the district he had represented as a congressman. He closed with these words: "So I come here tonight. I thank you for your past support. I ask you to join us tomorrow . . . I ask you to join us in all the tomorrows yet to come, in building America, moving America, picking this country of ours up and sending it into the sixties." (JFK Library.)

41

An enthusiastic supporter in Ware, Massachusetts, used his car as a billboard of support for JFK. Ware is located in Hampshire County in west central Massachusetts. Kennedy carried his home state with 60.2 percent of the vote. Massachusetts did not give Kennedy his largest plurality, no doubt due to the presence of popular Massachusetts native and its former senator Henry Cabot Lodge on the Republican ticket. (JFK Library.)

Jack and Jackie voted in Boston on the morning of November 8 and then headed home to Hyannis Port to wait for America's decision. The entire Kennedy clan gathered where they had been gathering for four decades. Here, the candidate, his wife, and daughter take a walk as they wait to learn if their next home will be 1600 Pennsylvania Avenue. (JFK Library.)

The 1960 election was one of the closest in American history. Kennedy went to bed at 3:30 a.m. and awoke six hours later victorious. After noon, Richard Nixon sent a congratulatory telegram. Kennedy made his first public appearance as president-elect at the armory building in downtown Hyannis (above), where a crowd had been gathering all morning. He intoned the gathering, "I ask your help . . . and I can assure you that every degree of mind and spirit that I possess will be devoted to the long-range interests of the United States and to the cause of freedom around the world. So now my wife and I prepare for a new administration and for a new baby." The president-elect and his wife (below, left) receive the well wishes of the gathered crowd as they leave the armory for home. John F. Kennedy Jr. was born 16 days later. (Both, JFK Library.)

On January 9, 1960, Kennedy addressed the Massachusetts State Legislature: "I am not here to bid farewell to Massachusetts . . . I have been guided by the standard John Winthrop set before his shipmates on the flagship Arbela 331 years ago, as they too faced the task of building a government on a new and perilous frontier . . . We must always consider . . . we shall be seen as a city upon a hill . . . The eyes of all people are upon us." (JFK Library.)

Old friends and supporters were not forgotten, as William and Mary Kelly of East Boston eye their invitation to Kennedy's inauguration. Kelly family folklore tells of the times Congressman Jack Kennedy would spend Sunday afternoons at the Kelly home in East Boston. It was said he would arrive from the Cape and read the Sunday paper and have dinner before catching a plane back to Washington. (Photograph by Mary McIntosh.)

Three

PRESIDENT KENNEDY AT HOME IN NEW ENGLAND

John F. Kennedy was the first president born in the 20th century. At 43, only Teddy Roosevelt was a younger chief executive, and JFK, his alluring 31-year-old wife, and their two beautiful children captivated the nation and indeed the world.

He was president for 1,037 days, encompassing 119 weekends, of which 46 were spent in New England; he spent 33 weekends in his beloved Hyannis Port, 12 in Newport, and 1 on St. Johns Island in Maine. And there were a few weekends when President Kennedy sailed from Newport to Hyannis Port. There were also visits home for campaigning for Democratic candidates, commencement addresses, fundraising dinners, celebrations, and dedications.

His home state marked him, and he explained how before the Massachusetts State Legislature: "The enduring qualities of Massachusetts—the common threads woven by the Pilgrim and the Puritan, the fisherman and the farmer, the Yankee and the immigrant . . . are an indelible part of my life, my convictions, my view of the past and my hopes for the future." Ever mindful of history and his place in it, he visited Boston in search of a place for his presidential library to house his archives when his term was ended. When that term came to its abrupt and tragic end, his home in Massachusetts was considered for his final resting place.

In a life that Jackie described to Arthur Schlesinger as "terrifically nomadic," the Kennedys were always on the go. With an apartment on Bowdoin Street in Boston—their legal voting address—and later a home in Georgetown, there is little doubt that Hyannis Port was his true home. He grew up there, and it was there where he developed his great love of the sea. He said of the Cape, "I always come back to the Cape and walk on the beach when I have a tough decision to make. The Cape is the one place I can think, and be alone." In 1992, at a reception at the JFK Museum in Hyannis, Sen. Ted Kennedy said, "The time President Kennedy spent in Hyannis Port during his youth and presidency were among the happiest days of his life." There was no more indelible mark made upon him than Hyannis Port and sailing.

JFK's first trip to New England as president came on his birthday weekend of May 27, 1961. After two days of rest and relaxation on the Cape, he flew into Boston's Logan Airport for a trip to celebrate his 44th birthday at the Commonwealth Armory in Boston, where he accepted a slice of birthday cake from one of the event's chefs. (JFK Library.)

President Kennedy and his family spent 16 weekends in Hyannis Port during the summer of 1961. Each of those weekends included a cruise on the *Marlin*, which doubled as a "conference room." JFK and defense secretary Robert McNamara walk to board for a conference at sea. (JFK Library.)

Although the first family spent every summer weekend of 1961 in Hyannis Port and ventured to Newport in the month of October, there are few photographs of them "at play" this first presidential summer. The speculative reasons include the first lady's passion to shield her children as much as possible from the omnipresent press, the president's desire to not "flaunt" his life of privilege, and their adjustment to the presidency. Images of the first couple on their way to church, however, abound. The above photograph shows them heading to mass at St. Francis Xavier Church in Hyannis Port on a September Sunday morning. A month later, White House photographer Robert Knudsen captured them arriving at St. Mary's Church in Newport, Rhode Island. (Above, JFK Library.)

On a 1961 September day that included the first lady waterskiing, a sail on the *Honey Fitz* (the presidential boat), and a trip to Bailey's Beach, the first family sat for a portrait session with Robert Knudsen. The site was the stairs inside the Hammersmith Farm estate. It was eight Septembers earlier when Jackie had thrown her bridal bouquet from the very same stairwell (as noted on page 34). (Knudsen.)

On June 11, 1962, JFK gave the commencement address at Yale University in New Haven, Connecticut, where he was presented an honorary degree. Yale, the Ivy League rival of the president's alma mater, Harvard, prompted him to open his remarks with, "It might be said now that I have the best of both worlds, a Harvard education and a Yale degree." (Knudsen.)

Above, on July 29, 1962, JFK, nephew Steven Smith Jr. (center), and friend Charles Spaulding (right) prepare the *Victura* for a sail in Lewis Bay off Hyannis Port, which included passengers Elizabeth Spaulding, the Spauldings' daughters Libby and Josie, as well as Jackie and Caroline. *Victura* came into Kennedy's life when he was a 15-year-old student at Choate. *Victura*, meaning "about to conquer," was a lifelong "friend" to JFK and, indeed, the entire family. She was a part of their competitive spirit and joyful times, and in times of tragedy and sadness, she brought solace. In his book *Victura*, James Graham wrote, "Whatever the lofty position a Kennedy held, helicopters, airplanes and motorcades all eventually pointed back to Hyannis Port in time for sailing races." Today, the *Victura* spends her summers on the lawn of the JFK Library, overlooking East Boston, once represented by Congressman John F. Kennedy. (Both, Stoughton.)

On Monday morning, July 30, 1962, it was back to work for President Kennedy and his attorney general. Before departing Hyannis Port, Robert Kennedy poses with children, from left to right, David, Kerry, Michael, and Courtney. Behind, JFK Jr. expresses his displeasure that his dad has to return to work. Ann Gargan is holding Junior as his father says goodbye. (Stoughton.)

During the summer of 1962, the first family rented the Squaw Island home of Morton Downey. Only a half mile away from the Kennedy Compound, it provided the president with more privacy from the swarms of press photographers and tourists, which flooded Hyannis hoping for a peek at the Kennedys. This photograph captures a windblown moment on the Downey porch on August 4, 1962. (Stoughton.)

On August 10, JFK arrived in the rain at the US Navy base in Brunswick, Maine, for the Navy Summer Festival. Greeting the crowd, he said, "Whether it shines or rains, I am delighted to be in this state and on the ocean." Following his welcome, he walked over to the Blue Angel pilots, signed an inscription, and then took a photograph with each one of them. (Knudsen.)

The president stayed at the Johns Island home (the only home on the island) of former heavyweight champ Gene Tunney. In his book *John F. Kennedy, Man of the Sea*, Kennedy's naval aide Tazewell Shepard wrote of JFK's historical interest, "In these waters . . . During the War of 1812 . . . American ship *Enterprise* . . . captured the British *Boxer*. Both Captains were killed and were buried side by side in Portland." (Knudsen.)

President Kennedy and his sister Pat Lawford leave Our Lady of Peace Church. Today, the church website includes the words of parishioner Josephine Carbone who wrote: "We enjoyed the visit because it gave us a day unlike any other. It cast a spell here that has lingered. It brought out our best . . . It was a day . . . which illuminated our times. It was a day well worth remembering." (Stoughton.)

Back on the *Horsewhip II*, JFK waits as the crew prepares to shove off. Paul "Red" Fay is pointing out something to Tazewell Shepard (left of Fay) and Pat Lawford as local boaters move to get a closer look. Today, inside the church, this visit is memorialized in two places. A plaque on the rear wall pictures the president on the church steps, and the pew in which he sat is marked with another plaque. (Knudsen.)

At 12:30 p.m., the president's party set sail on the Coast Guard Yacht *Manitou*. JFK was at the tiller for most of the 50-mile sail along Maine's coast. On board are, from left to right, Charles Spaulding, Paul "Red" Fay, Peter Lawford, JFK, and James Reed (behind JFK). Reed, a Maine native, served as JFK's assistant secretary of the treasury. The two met in 1943 on a troop transport ship bound for the South Pacific. (Knudsen.)

The president left the tiller for a bit, taking to the bow of the ship to enjoy a cigar and smell the sea. In an oral interview for the JFK Library, James Reed said: "He wanted to sail the boat himself . . . It was a great time, he had a marvelous time, he got away from everything . . . he just loved it. I think it was one of the best weekends he ever had." (Knudsen.)

There is perhaps no photograph that embodies the essence of John F. Kennedy more than this one of him at the tiller of the *Manitou*. It portrays the president, a man of the sea, exuding leadership not only at the helm of *Manitou*, but at the helm of the ship of state as well. Tazewell Shepard wrote of the president's weekend sailing the rocky coast of Maine, "He filled his lungs with fresh sea air and exhilarated in the bracing wind and salt spray. It was the happiest of times . . . Anyone who saw him there would have had no doubt that the president felt keenly the enchantment of the sea." In the forward to Shepard's book, Ted Kennedy wrote, "President Kennedy loved the sea with a mariners love." (Knudsen.)

The weekend ended with a clam bake on Johns Island; Red Fay remembered that "at 5 pm the Blue Angels came over treetop . . . all six of them . . . going about 500 miles an hour . . . no higher than . . . 30 feet off the top of the trees . . . trailing red, white and blue smoke streamers. They went through all their acrobatics above the president and finished by rocking their wings as they went by . . . it was a most memorable thing." (Knudsen.)

Hammersmith Farm was the home in which Jacqueline Bouvier Kennedy grew up. The 28-room mansion was built on 48 acres in 1887 for John Auchincloss, the great-great-grandfather of Jackie's stepfather Hugh. It was the site of the Kennedy/Bouvier wedding, and in September 1962, it earned the nickname of the "Summer White House." (Knudsen.)

Sunday morning, August 26, 1962, began with mass at St. Francis Xavier Church in Hyannis and then a ride on Marine One to Hammersmith Farm in Newport, where the president was greeted by his son John on the front lawn. Standing from left to right by Kennedy are naval aide Tazewell Shepard, mother-in-law Janet Auchincloss (white dress), sister-in-law Janet Auchincloss (blue pants), and father-in-law Hugh Auchincloss. (Knudsen.)

That afternoon, the Auchincloss family enjoyed a sail with the president on the *Manitou*. At the tiller, while JFK enjoys a cigar, is his sister-in-law Janet Auchincloss. Identifiable are JFK's mother-in-law Janet (white dress) and John Kerry behind her. Kerry (18 years old in this photograph) was dating Janet at the time and would go on to represent Massachusetts in the US Senate and serve as Pres. Barack Obama's secretary of state from 2013 to 2017. (Knudsen.)

The weekend included exploring the New England seas on three different vessels. In this photograph, the president took a Sunday cruise on Rhode Island Sound on the *Manitou* that included, from left to right, Nuala Pell (wearing a white kerchief) and her daughter Julie, Countess Consuelo Crespi (in a red sweater), Janet Auchincloss (in the center wearing white), Rhode Island senator Claiborne Pell (gesturing), Sybil Miller (in a gray sweater) and Jamie Auchincloss. (Knudsen.)

On Friday night, September 14, Pres. and First Lady Kennedy were the guests of honor at Newport's famous Breakers mansion to officially kick off the 1962 America's Cup yacht races. The black-tie affair was hosted by Australian ambassador Howard (next to JFK) and Lady Beale (wearing an orange dress). (Knudsen.)

In his opening remarks, JFK, seen here with Jackie during dinner, joked about the historical connection between Australia and Rhode Island. "In the 1790s . . . American ships, mostly from Rhode Island, began to call regularly at New South Wales . . . their cargos, I regret to say, consisted mainly of gin and rum." The races began the following day, and the president was welcomed aboard the USS *Joseph P Kennedy Jr* by Captain Mikhalevsky (below, far left) and presented with a model and a signed schematic of the ship by Electrician's Mate First Class Gilbert Olsen. In his remarks, JFK said, "The Kennedy means a good deal to all of us . . . My sister took part in the commissioning . . . my brother Robert served on it . . . it was built in Fore River Massachusetts . . . it has been the greatest source of satisfaction to all of us." (Both, Knudsen.)

On board, the president, first lady, and their guests survey the horizon as the race unfolds. Behind the president are, from left to right, Hugh Auchincloss (wearing binoculars around neck), Paul Fay (lifting binoculars), Jamie Auchincloss, Janet Auchincloss, John Kerry (the 2004 Democratic presidential candidate), Pierre Salinger (wearing pink jacket) and naval aide Tazewell Shepard. This photograph appeared in Tazewell Shepard's 1965 book *John F. Kennedy Man of the Sea*, but Kerry was not identified. (Knudsen.)

Spectators settle in around the president to watch the US yacht *Weatherly* battle the Australian vessel the *Gretel*. This race marked the first time since the America Cup's inception in 1851 that the challengers did not come from Great Britain or Canada. Surrounding the first couple are, from left to right, Massachusetts senator Ben Smith, Tazewell Shepard, Paul Fay, Hugh Auchincloss (shading his eyes), and James Reed. (Knudsen.)

In the 3 hours, 13 minutes, and 46 seconds it took for the *Weatherly* to vanquish *Gretel* in the 14-mile inaugural race of the 1962 America's Cup, President Kennedy and Jackie were captured by White House photographer Robert Knudsen alone amidst the throng of senators, congressman, dignitaries, family, and friends aboard the USS *Joseph P. Kennedy Jr.* (Both, Knudsen.)

The president confers with his press secretary Pierre Salinger (wearing pink), who appears to be taking notes while Jackie Kennedy enjoys a little banter with Franklin Roosevelt Jr. (standing, wearing binoculars around his neck) and Nuala Pell (with her back to camera). Roosevelt served as JFK's undersecretary of commerce, and Pell's husband was Rhode Island senator Claiborne Pell. (Knudsen.)

There were no races the following two days; however, this did not keep the president from the sea, as there was sailing on the *Honey Fitz* and the *Manitou* on both days. In this photograph, JFK and Jackie entertain Giovanni Agnelli (behind JFK) and his wife, Princess Marella (wearing pink pants, speaking with Jackie) aboard the *Manitou*. Agnelli, the head of Fiat, was considered the richest man in modern Italian history. (Knudsen.)

The race resumed on Tuesday, September 18, and in this photograph of the deck of the USS *Joseph P. Kennedy Jr.*, there are various conversations taking place among the guests as one of them enjoys a nap. All the while, the president leans forward to chat with his daughter Caroline and young Count Brando Crespi, the son of *Vogue* editor Countess Crespi, and Count Rodolpho Crespi. (Knudsen.)

The president returned to Washington late on September 19. He put in a 15-hour workday on September 20 before arriving back in Newport at 11:38 p.m. The following day, on September 21, he cruised on the *Honey Fitz* from Newport to Hyannis Port, and on September 22, he boarded the USS *Joseph P. Kennedy Jr.* for the fourth of the America's Cup races. (Knudsen.)

JFK and Jackie share a word while Jean Kennedy Smith (far left) eyeballs the *Weatherly* and her husband, Steve, adjusts his binoculars. The America's Cup is the oldest international sporting event in the world. (Knudsen.)

Presidential press secretary Pierre Salinger shares a laugh with his boss on the deck of the USS *Joseph P. Kennedy Jr.* during the fourth race of the America's Cup race. Noting the difference in the dress of the president and Salinger (a California native), it is quite likely that Salinger is receiving some good-natured ribbing for his "over protection" from the elements. (Knudsen.)

The president follows the action of the race while standing next to past New York Yacht Club commodore Harold Vanderbilt, the great-grandson of shipping and railroad tycoon Cornelius Vanderbilt. Vanderbilt crewed America's Cup winners in 1930, 1934, and 1937 and was elected to the America's Cup Hall of Fame in 1993. Jean and Steve Smith (wearing leather jackets) watch the action. (Knudsen.)

Mingling on the deck, JFK talks with unidentified guests while Jackie engages in a conversation with writer George Plimpton. Plimpton was at the start of what would become a very successful career launched by a series of books in which he trained in a sport and then participated in exhibition games as a professional. In 1963, he penned a privately published book about Caroline Kennedy, *Go Caroline*. (Knudsen.)

With the races behind them, the president and first lady welcomed Mohammad Ayub Khan, president of Pakistan, to America at Quonset Point Naval Station in Rhode Island. Behind President Khan is Angier Biddle Duke, protocol officer for the US Department of State. Jackie Kennedy and Khan had a mutual admiration for each other, which began upon their meeting in July 1961. (Knudsen.)

After posing for pictures, the first couple escorted President Kahn and his entourage to Marine One on the lawn. The following day, Jackie Kennedy and President Kahn rode together to Virginia. Kahn had presented her with a horse on the first lady's trip to Pakistan in March 1962, and Clint Hill wrote, "Mrs. Kennedy was eager to show Ayub Kahn how delighted she was with his gift of a horse named Sardar." (Knudsen.)

On April 20, 1963, the president made the first trip of the year to his home state. The occasion was the centennial celebration of Boston College in Chestnut Hill. His speech outlined his vision for universities and the role he saw them play in America. In a theme that ran through his administration from the outset, he said, "They should be dedicated to the nation's service." (Stoughton.)

Making his way back to the airport, the president stops to view the future site of the JFK Library. He gestures toward the proposed area, showing US archivist Dr. Wayne Grover (beside JFK) and Harvard vice president Lewis Wiggins (holding hat) where the library will be. In the distance are two Harvard landmark towers, the Dunster House (left) and Eliot Hall (right). Today, across the street from Eliot Hall in Harvard Square is the John F. Kennedy School of Government. (Stoughton.)

JFK's first 1963 trip to Hyannis—May 10—was a working weekend at the president's newly rented summer home Brambletyde on Squaw Island. Just around the corner from the family compound, it provided far more privacy for the first family, as tourists had literally overrun the area in increasing numbers. The guest was Canadian prime minister Lester Pearson, who is seen disembarking Marine One. The pair posed for photographs on the porch upon their arrival. (Both, Stoughton.)

JFK did not return to Hyannis Port until the Fourth of July. In a most rare photograph, Jackie embraces the president, welcoming him home. The first couple was not known for open displays of affection, particularly in the presence of cameras. Caroline is watching her brother pick up something as Lem Billings (left) walks along. Below, Jackie holds John Jr. as the family awaits a fireworks display. (Both, Stoughton.)

The weekend included, as always, sailing of one sort or another. In these two images, the president and crew launch a toy sailboat. The boat was a gift to John Jr. from Italian president Antonio Segni. In the photograph above, JFK gives instructions to his crew of Lem Billings and Caroline, while his brother Ted and a secret service agent look on. Below, JFK and Caroline survey the results of a job well done as Lem Billings returns to shore. (Both, Stoughton.)

JFK was a far better than average golfer, and press secretary Pierre Salinger (top swinging) was not. However, after hearing that Salinger had improved, Kennedy suggested they play. On a late July weekend, they teed up at the Hyannis Port Club. Salinger wrote in his book *With Kennedy*, "I teed up my ball . . . took a couple of nervous practice swings and let it fly. The ball flew off the toe of my club . . . and hit the clubhouse." Below, Salinger gets some pointers from the boss, recalling, "I hit a good drive on the second hole." However, his second shot "came within two feet of hitting the President in the head," prompting the comment from secret service agent Roy Kellerman, "I can protect him from the crowd, but who's going to protect him from you?" (Both, Stoughton.)

JFK leads (in order behind him) Pierre Salinger, Lem Billings, and David Ormsby-Gore across the bridge connecting the tee to the green. The president and Ormsby-Gore teamed up against Salinger and Charles Spaulding (wearing a blue shirt in the distance), and the Salinger team was on the short end of every hole. The match was mercifully interrupted when a military helicopter landed next to the 14th fairway, carrying Under Secretary Averill Harriman (left) and Secretary of State Dean Rusk (second from right). They had arrived to discuss the recently agreed upon details of the Nuclear Test Ban Treaty. From the helicopter, Kennedy placed a call to golf pro Tom Niblet to cancel a lesson; "Something came up," he told Niblet. JFK stands between Harriman and Rusk back at Brambletyde as they pose for the press before going to work. (Both, Stoughton.)

Virtually every day in Hyannis Port involved time on the seas of Nantucket Sound, either sailing the *Victura*, cruising aboard the presidential yacht *Honey Fitz*, or spending time on the Kennedy family boat the *Marlin*. Above, the president enjoys a cigar and the conversation of his daughter Caroline, niece Maria Shriver, and brother-in-law Stephen Smith as the *Honey Fitz* heads out to sea. In the background is the Kennedy home. Very often, a boat trip involved dropping an anchor and taking a swim. Below, from left to right, JFK, Maria, and Caroline dove off the boat to do just that. (Both, Stoughton.)

At 5:26 p.m. on August 2, 1963, the president's helicopter, Marine One, landed on the front lawn of the home of Kennedy family patriarch Joseph Kennedy. The president disembarked followed by his brother and attorney general Robert and his brother-in-law and head of the Peace Corps Sargent Shriver. Kids swarmed the front lawn, with each running full speed to their respective dads. Following kisses and hugs, it was time for a group photograph with daddy/Uncle Jack, which was accomplished with the kids showing varying degrees of interest and emotions. The next day, on the *Honey Fitz*, JFK, Jackie, and Anita Fay exchange good wishes with, from left to right, Ethel Kennedy, Mary Kerry Kennedy, Robert Kennedy, Joseph Kennedy, and Kennedy cousin Ann Gargan aboard the *Marlin*. Despite his limitations due to a stroke, Amb. Joseph Kennedy loved time spent on the water. (Both, Stoughton.)

In these two photographs, JFK, Anita and Red Fay (above) and Jackie (left) are engrossed in their reading. The president was rarely far away from something to read, and the deck of the *Honey Fitz* was no exception. Fay, whom JFK met in the South Pacific during World War II remained a close friend of the president throughout his life, and he served as his undersecretary of the Navy. Among Jackie's favorite subjects were novels and diaries from the courts of Europe. She is eight months pregnant in this photograph, with the baby due some five weeks hence. In his book *The Pleasure of His Company*, Fay wrote about Kennedy's affinity for Cape Cod: "He relaxed most thoroughly . . . in a place at Squaw Island (Brambletyde) . . . this weathered, comfortable, sprawling structure . . . seemed to be everything he ever wanted . . . in a . . . home." (Both, Stoughton.)

In the photograph above, Kennedy and Paul "Red" Fay chat with club pro Tom Niblet before teeing off. In the photograph below, the pair make their way to the next hole. JFK signed this picture for Fay with "a cheerful loser, from a happy winner." Fay wrote of Kennedy's passion for golf. On a foggy February morning, JFK's secretary Evelyn Lincoln called him to come by at 11:45 a.m. and bring his clubs. The fog precluded a match, but the president said, "Why don't we go out here in the Rose Garden and hit some!" After hitting irons for a while, JFK asked, "If you hit a driver . . . on the screws . . . do you think you could get one off the grounds . . . I began to swing in earnest . . . balls flew over the Rose Garden . . . over the trees," disappearing in the fog, leaving the president and undersecretary never knowing if Fay succeeded. (Both, Stoughton.)

On the morning of August 5, Monday, the president departed Hyannis Port for Washington. There was a ritual at the Hyannis Port compound when the president departed. His father was wheeled onto the front porch to watch Marine One lift off for Otis Air Force Base, where the president would board Air Force One. In these two photographs, the president kisses his father goodbye, who in turn kisses his grandson goodbye. JFK Jr. would often take the ride in the helicopter to Otis. (Both, Stoughton.)

On August 7, 1963, Patrick Bouvier Kennedy was born, delivered by an emergency caesarean section. For 39 hours, the president shuffled back and forth between Boston (above) and Hyannis, and after a valiant battle, little Patrick succumbed. Powers wrote, "Around two o'clock in morning . . . Patrick's condition was taking a bad turn . . . I awakened the president . . . While waiting for the elevator [he] noticed . . . a small child who had been severely burned . . . He borrowed a pen and slip of paper . . . and wrote a note of sympathy and encouragement to the mother . . . Two hours later the strain on . . . the baby's heart became unbearable and he died. 'He put up a good fight . . . He was a beautiful baby' JFK said . . . He went upstairs to [his] room . . . sat on the bed and wept . . . The president went to the helicopter . . . and flew to Otis . . . where he spent an hour alone with Jackie." In the photograph below, Pierre Salinger announces the death of Patrick to the press at Otis Air Force Base. (Above, JFK Library; below, Stoughton.)

On August 14, Jackie was released from the hospital at Otis Air Force Base. The president took Marine One to Otis (left) and then back to their Squaw Island home (below), where Caroline snuggles up with Wolf, one of the eight Kennedy family dogs. There is a sadness to Caroline's face, no doubt brought on by the loss of her new baby brother. Ted Kennedy wrote in *True Compass*, "Jack kept stoic about his loss, but those of us closest to him could see how he suffered . . . When he and Jackie returned to the Cape . . . he invited me over . . . we swam and . . . walked on the beach. Jack was absorbed in everything . . . his small son was doing. In the few months left to him . . . Jack's greatest concern was for his wife's and children's welfare." (Both, Stoughton.)

Saturday, August 24 brought rain and another day inside. Even though a late summer chill was in the air, the rain was gone on Sunday, which meant the Kennedys were on the move. In the image at right, JFK reads his Sunday paper while cruising on the *Honey Fitz* before he and Caroline take in the sights of Nantucket Sound (below). (Both, Stoughton.)

On Monday morning, August 26, the sun was shining, and it was time for daddy to return to work. In the photograph above, Caroline gives him some last-minute instructions as they make their way towards Marine One while her brother John rushes ahead. Cousin Sydney Lawford is in front of Caroline, and cousin David Kennedy walks behind. From left to right, secret service men Sam Sullivan Jerry Behn, and Tom Wells follow along. In the photograph below, Uncle Jack says goodbye to nieces and nephews before climbing aboard. (Both, Stoughton.)

It was a short week in Washington, and the president returned on Thursday eve for Labor Day weekend. The three days found him cruising on the *Honey Fitz* with family and friends, and as always, there was time for reading. A speed reader who could absorb 1,200 words a minute, JFK was, according to his wife, always reading. In Jackie's interview with Arthur Schlesinger, she said this about her husband's propensity for the written word: "He read walking, he'd read at the table, at meals, he'd read after dinner, he'd read in the bathtub, he'd read—prop open a book on his desk—on his bureau—while doing his tie . . . He really read all the times you don't think you have time to read." In the photograph below with JFK and Jackie are two unidentified women and brother-in-law Steve Smith. (Both, Stoughton.)

A part of the Hyannis Port weekend routine would often include a walk or golf cart ride to Lorainia's Toy and Book Shop in Hyannis. On this Labor Day weekend, Paul Fay (below, left) joined the Kennedys and a secret service agent on the walk. The president is carrying a stuffed animal while his son carries a toy helicopter. Fay had a special relationship with John Jr., as he would regularly throw him up into the air and catch him—something his dad was unable to do because of his chronic back pain. Throughout the years, there have been conflicting reports regarding the use of "John-John" as a nickname for JFK Jr. In his oral history for the JFK Library, Paul Fay said President Kennedy "called him John-John all the time." (Both, Stoughton.)

Television history was made on September 2, 1963, when CBS news anchor Walter Cronkite traveled to Hyannis Port to interview President Kennedy on the Brambletyde lawn. CBS had made the decision to expand the *CBS Evening News* to a half hour from the standard 15 minutes and used this interview with JFK to inaugurate that format. Just five days earlier, Martin Luther King had delivered his "I Have a Dream" speech in Washington, DC. Cronkite's first question was related to the march and the response throughout the country. JFK responded that it was "an impressive manifestation of a strong desire of a good many responsible citizens for equal treatment . . . I'm hopeful . . . both parties . . . will commit themselves . . . to the . . . equality of opportunity . . . I would be surprised if the republican party, the party of Lincoln . . . did not also support the right of every citizen for equal opportunity." Eighty percent of the Republicans in the House and Senate did just that. (Both, Stoughton.)

Cruising off the coast of Hyannis Port on September 7, 1963, President Kennedy enjoys an ice-cream cone aboard the *Honey Fitz*. Ice cream was on the list of JFK's favorite foods. (Stoughton.)

Uncle Jack waits in a golf cart after a cruise on the *Honey Fitz*. Lem Billings puts JFK Jr. on his shoulders while Kennedy nephew David Kennedy and his sister Mary Kerry wait to get going. Mary Kerry seems to be getting a point across to her brother as Jackie makes her way to the cart. (Stoughton.)

A gathering of the Kennedys always involved song, and of course, it would be no different on the night seen above. "September Song" was a favorite of the president, and he sang it from the time he was a youngster with his mother on the piano. "Heart of my Heart" was another family favorite. In these photographs, the family performs for their father (below, far left) in celebration of his 75th birthday, and it is clear he is delighted by their performance. The president sits below to the right, and Jackie wears white on the edge of the couch. (Both, Stoughton.)

The following weekend, longtime friends Ben Bradlee and his wife, Toni, accompanied JFK on Air Force One to Newport. Bradlee wrote in his book *Conversations with Kennedy*, "This was the first time we had seen Jackie since the death of little Patrick . . . she greeted JFK with . . . the most enthusiastic embrace we had ever seen them give each other." The president engaged in all the family activities that marked a Kennedy family weekend in New England. Seen above, President Kennedy took a swim with John Jr. in the pool at Bailey's Beach. After the morning swim, it was a drive to Fort Adams, where the commander in chief boarded the *Honey Fitz* for some time on the sea. Saluted as he boards, he was followed on board by Jackie and the Bradlees. (Both, Knudsen.)

Golf was a part of the weekend as the president (seen here teeing off) and Jackie were joined by Ben Bradlee (waiting to hit); his wife, Toni; and caddy Ronnie Hogan. The Bradlees were neighbors in Georgetown, and Ben Bradlee was the Washington bureau chief for *Newsweek* during Kennedy's presidency. He would later become editor of the *Washington Post*, which ultimately unveiled the Watergate cover-up, leading to Pres. Richard Nixon's resignation in 1974. (Knudsen.)

About 200 people watched the president play golf, and he visited with them when the round was over. On the way back to Hammersmith Farm, Kennedy stopped the car to chat with three nuns who had been part of the crowd. Bradlee wrote, "He wanted to know all about them . . . What order they were in . . . where they worked" and then "we were all startled to hear, Jackie here always wanted to be a nun." (Knudsen.)

On Saturday October 19, 1963, President Kennedy left Washington for Dow Air Force Base in Bangor, Maine, and then he was on to the University of Maine in nearby Orono. The president received an honorary law degree, and in his remarks, he spoke on Soviet/US relations, intoning, "While maintaining our preparedness for war, let us explore every avenue for peace . . . until the world we pass on to our children is truly safe for diversity." (Stoughton.)

A short flight to Boston and a trip to his alma mater for the Harvard/Columbia football game at Harvard Stadium was on the agenda. From left to right in the row with Kennedy are White House appointment secretary Kenny O'Donnell (a Harvard graduate), special assistant Dave Powers (in the sunglasses), Maine senator Ed Muskie, JFK, and special assistant Larry O'Brien. The game ended in a 3-3 tie. (Stoughton.)

JFK was not present at end of the game. Dave Powers wrote, "Toward the end of the first half . . . he turned to me and said, 'I want to go to Patrick's grave and I want to go there alone.' " Arrangements were made, and Powers and Kenny O'Donnell accompanied him to the cemetery. "He seems so alone here," JFK remarked. By December, Patrick and his father were together in Arlington National Cemetery. (JFK Library.)

October 19 ended with a Democratic fundraiser at the Boston Armory. From left to right are Speaker John McCormack, dinner cochairman Tom White, JFK, and Sen. Ted Kennedy. The president bantered with his kid brother; "I want to express my appreciation to my brother Teddy for offering me his coat-tails." He added, "It's a constant source of pride . . . that I come from this state . . . that I'm identified with this state." It was his last time in Boston. (Stoughton.)

After Sunday mass at Boston's St. Francis Xavier Church, Kennedy exchanged pleasantries with the priest (left) and an enthusiastic crowd greeted him (below). Dave Powers (left, wearing hat at far left) and JFK were bound for a day in Hyannis. The day marked the last time he sailed his beloved waters of Nantucket Sound. On Monday morning, he departed Hyannis Port for the last time. Upon leaving, JFK said goodbye to his dad; Dave Powers wrote, "The Ambassador was on the porch . . . The president went to him . . . and kissed him on the forehead . . . He started to the helicopter . . . turned, looked at his father and went back and kissed him a second time . . . When the president was inside the helicopter . . . he looked out at the figure in the wheel chair and his eyes filled with tears." It was the last time he saw his father. (Both, Stoughton.)

October 26, 1963, was the last time that John Kennedy set foot on New England soil. The event was the ground-breaking ceremony (right) for the Robert Frost Library at Amherst College in Massachusetts. It is serendipitous that this should be his last trip home, for Frost was Kennedy's favorite poet. The octogenarian poet and the young president forged a friendship late in the poet's life, and Frost recited a poem at Kennedy's inauguration. Delivering brief remarks, he said of Frost, "I was impressed with his toughness . . . He once said America's the country you leave only when you want to go out and lick another country . . . He once said to me not to let the Harvard in me get to be too important . . . Libraries are memories and in this library you will have the memory of an extraordinary American." Below is the moment when JFK left New England—forever. (Both, Stoughton.)

THE BOSTON HERALD

PRESIDENT KENNEDY ASSASSINATED

Lyndon Johnson Is Sworn In, Governor of Texas Wounded, Dallas Man Accused as Killer

Dazed Jackie Curbs Tears 'Til Trip Home

Gov. Connally Badly Wounded

3-Day Ritual Starts Today, Mass Monday

Nation's Tragedy in Pictures and Stories

On Pages 2, 3, 4, 5, 6, 7, 8, 9, 10, 11, 12

New President: 'I'll Do My Best'

Peabody to Fly To Washington

A Shot to Nation's Heart

Officer Tippett Slain in Chase

Turn of Body Spared Life Of Connally

Johnson Escapes Any Injury

Brother Tec Sister Fly tc Parents' Sid

America Weeps Now—For Itself

Stay in Russia

Today's Herald

Stunned City Halts Normal Routine

On November 22, 1963, John F. Kennedy was riding in a motorcade in Dallas, Texas. Jackie sat next to him, and Texas governor John Connolly and his wife, Nellie, sat in front of them. At 12:31 p.m. CST, they were passing through Dealey Plaza on their way to a luncheon speech at the Texas Trade Mart when shots reigned down upon them, killing the president and wounding Connolly. (Author's collection.)

The American flag flies at half-mast outside the Hyannis Port home of John F. Kennedy on November 27, 1963, while a lonely worker makes his way across the yard. Flags flew at half-mast for 30 days following the president's assassination. (JFK Library.)

Presidential Gallup polling began during the administration of Harry Truman. Since its inception, there is no president who has achieved a higher average approval rating from the American people than John F. Kennedy. Throughout his administration, 70.1 percent of the American people approved of his performance. His popularity has extended beyond his life, as approximately four million visit his grave yearly. His legacy transcends across generations of Americans. In the 1990 photograph above, the great-grandchildren of William F. Kelly visit the birthplace of JFK at 83 Beals Street in Brookline, Massachusetts. In July 2015, twenty-five summers later, Kelly's great-great-grandchildren made the same visit, as seen at right. (Above, author's collection; right, Rachael Adams.)

BIBLIOGRAPHY

Bradlee, Benjamin. *Conversations with Kennedy*. New York: Norton and Company, 1975.

Dalleck, Robert. *An Unfinished Life, John F. Kennedy 1917–1963*. Boston: Little Brown & Company, 2003.

Fay, Paul. *The Pleasure of His Company*. New York: Harper and Row, 1965.

Graham, James. *Victura, The Kennedys a Sailboat and the Sea*. New Hampshire: University Press of New England, 2014.

Hill, Clint. *Mrs. Kennedy and Me*. New York: Gallery Books, 2012.

Kennedy, Edward. *True Compass, a memoir*. New York/Boston: Twelve, 2011.

Kennedy, Jacqueline. *Historic Conversations on life with John F. Kennedy*. New York: Hyperion, 2011.

Leaming, Barbara. *Mrs. Kennedy, the Missing History of the Kennedy Years*. New York: The Free Press, 2001.

O'Donnell, Kenneth, and David Powers. *Johnny We Hardly Knew Ye*. Boston: Little Brown & Company, 1970.

Parmet, Herbert. *Jack, the Struggles of John F. Kennedy*. New York: The Dial Press, 1980.

Salinger, Pierre. *With Kennedy*. Garden City, New York: Doubleday & Company, 1966.

Shepard Jr., Tazewell. *John F. Kennedy, Man of the Sea*. New York: William Morrow & Company 1965.

ABOUT THE ORGANIZATION

Founded in 1964, the John F. Kennedy Library Foundation provides private financial support to the JFK Library and museum. This public/private partnership works to bringing to fruition the mission as stated by Jacqueline Kennedy when she wrote, "It will be not only a memorial to President Kennedy but a living center of study of the times in which he lived, which will inspire the ideals of democracy and freedom in young people all over the world." To learn more about the foundation, contact them at:

John F. Kennedy Library Foundation
Columbia Point
Boston, Massachusetts, 02125

DISCOVER THOUSANDS OF LOCAL HISTORY BOOKS FEATURING MILLIONS OF VINTAGE IMAGES

Arcadia Publishing, the leading local history publisher in the United States, is committed to making history accessible and meaningful through publishing books that celebrate and preserve the heritage of America's people and places.

Find more books like this at
www.arcadiapublishing.com

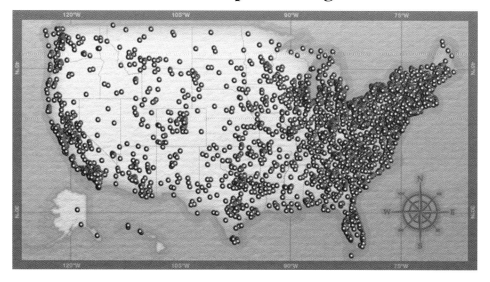

Search for your hometown history, your old stomping grounds, and even your favorite sports team.

Consistent with our mission to preserve history on a local level, this book was printed in South Carolina on American-made paper and manufactured entirely in the United States. Products carrying the accredited Forest Stewardship Council (FSC) label are printed on 100 percent FSC-certified paper.

MADE IN THE USA